EMMANUEL JOSEPH

Innovating with Integrity, Emotional Intelligence, Social Dynamics, and Ethical Business Growth

Copyright © 2025 by Emmanuel Joseph

All rights reserved. No part of this publication may be reproduced, stored or transmitted in any form or by any means, electronic, mechanical, photocopying, recording, scanning, or otherwise without written permission from the publisher. It is illegal to copy this book, post it to a website, or distribute it by any other means without permission.

First edition

This book was professionally typeset on Reedsy.
Find out more at reedsy.com

Contents

1. Chapter 1: The Foundations of Integrity in Innovation ... 1
2. Chapter 2: Emotional Intelligence: The Key to Ethical... ... 3
3. Chapter 3: Social Dynamics in the Workplace ... 5
4. Chapter 4: The Role of Ethical Decision-Making in Business... ... 7
5. Chapter 5: Building an Ethical Culture ... 9
6. Chapter 6: The Intersection of Emotional Intelligence and... ... 11
7. Chapter 7: The Importance of Trust in Ethical Business... ... 13
8. Chapter 8: Ethical Innovation in a Globalized World ... 15
9. Chapter 9: Ethical Marketing and Branding ... 17
10. Chapter 10: The Role of Corporate Governance in Ethical... ... 19
11. Chapter 11: Ethical Challenges in the Digital Age ... 21
12. Chapter 12: Ethical Leadership in Times of Crisis ... 23
13. Chapter 13: Innovation and Sustainability ... 25
14. Chapter 14: The Future of Work: Ethical Considerations ... 27
15. Chapter 15: The Role of Ethics in Research and Development ... 29
16. Chapter 16: The Role of Ethics in Corporate Strategy ... 31
17. Chapter 17: Ethical Business Growth: A Roadmap for the... ... 33
18. Chapter 18: Implementing Ethical Standards Across Global... ... 35
19. Chapter 19: Measuring the Impact of Ethical Practices ... 37
20. Chapter 20: The Future of Ethical Innovation ... 39

1

Chapter 1: The Foundations of Integrity in Innovation

Innovation thrives in an environment where integrity is upheld as a core value. In a world driven by rapid technological advancements and ever-evolving market demands, maintaining ethical standards can be challenging. However, integrity is the cornerstone of sustainable growth and long-term success. This chapter explores the significance of integrity in innovation, emphasizing the need for transparency, honesty, and accountability in business practices. By setting a strong ethical foundation, organizations can foster trust among stakeholders and create a positive reputation that attracts both customers and talent.

Moreover, integrity in innovation goes beyond just adhering to rules and regulations; it involves a commitment to doing what is right even when no one is watching. This moral compass guides decision-making processes and ensures that businesses prioritize the well-being of society and the environment. Companies that integrate integrity into their innovation strategies are better positioned to navigate complex ethical dilemmas and make choices that align with their values and mission.

Furthermore, the role of leadership in promoting integrity cannot be overstated. Leaders who lead by example and demonstrate ethical behavior inspire their teams to follow suit. By cultivating a culture of integrity, leaders can empower employees to voice their concerns, share ideas, and collaborate in a safe and respectful environment. This chapter delves into various leadership styles that foster ethical innovation and highlights the importance of consistent communication and reinforcement of ethical standards.

Lastly, integrity in innovation is not a one-time effort but an ongoing commitment. Organizations must continuously evaluate and refine their ethical frameworks to address emerging challenges and opportunities. By embedding integrity into the fabric of their operations, businesses can build resilience and adaptability, ensuring that their innovative endeavors contribute to a better future for all stakeholders.

2

Chapter 2: Emotional Intelligence: The Key to Ethical Leadership

Emotional intelligence (EI) is a critical component of ethical leadership and innovation. Leaders with high EI are adept at understanding and managing their emotions, as well as recognizing and influencing the emotions of others. This chapter explores the connection between emotional intelligence and ethical decision-making, highlighting how EI enables leaders to navigate complex interpersonal dynamics and foster a positive organizational culture.

One of the key aspects of emotional intelligence is self-awareness. Leaders who possess self-awareness are better equipped to identify their strengths and weaknesses, allowing them to make informed decisions and seek feedback for continuous improvement. This chapter discusses various strategies for developing self-awareness, including reflective practices, mindfulness, and seeking diverse perspectives. By enhancing self-awareness, leaders can align their actions with their values and ensure that their innovation efforts are grounded in integrity.

Empathy, another crucial component of emotional intelligence, plays a significant role in ethical leadership. Empathetic leaders can understand and appreciate the perspectives and experiences of others, which fosters inclusivity and collaboration. This chapter examines the importance of empathy in building strong relationships with stakeholders, addressing conflicts, and making ethical decisions that consider the well-being of all parties involved. Through real-life examples and practical exercises, readers will learn how to cultivate empathy and integrate it into their leadership style.

In addition to self-awareness and empathy, emotional intelligence encompasses social skills that facilitate effective communication and relationship-building. Leaders with strong social skills can inspire and motivate their teams, navigate challenging conversations, and build a cohesive and resilient organizational culture. This chapter provides insights into various social skills, such as active listening, conflict resolution, and team-building, that are essential for ethical leadership and innovation. By developing these skills, leaders can create an environment where integrity and innovation thrive.

Ultimately, emotional intelligence is a lifelong journey of self-improvement and growth. This chapter encourages leaders to invest in their emotional development and seek opportunities for learning and growth. By prioritizing emotional intelligence, leaders can drive ethical innovation and create a positive impact on their organizations and society.

3

Chapter 3: Social Dynamics in the Workplace

Social dynamics play a pivotal role in shaping workplace culture and driving innovation. Understanding the complex interplay of relationships, power structures, and communication patterns is essential for fostering a collaborative and inclusive environment. This chapter delves into the intricacies of social dynamics in the workplace and their impact on ethical business growth.

One of the key aspects of social dynamics is the concept of psychological safety. When employees feel safe to express their ideas, take risks, and voice concerns without fear of retribution, innovation flourishes. This chapter explores strategies for creating psychological safety, including promoting open communication, encouraging diversity of thought, and addressing biases and power imbalances. By fostering a psychologically safe environment, organizations can harness the collective intelligence of their teams and drive ethical innovation.

In addition to psychological safety, social capital is another critical factor in workplace dynamics. Social capital refers to the networks of relationships and trust that exist within an organization. This chapter examines the importance of building and nurturing social capital through team-building activities, mentoring programs, and cross-functional collaboration. By strengthening social capital, organizations can enhance cooperation, knowledge sharing, and innovation.

Moreover, the role of diversity and inclusion in social dynamics cannot be overstated. Diverse teams bring a wide range of perspectives, experiences, and ideas, which can lead to more creative and innovative solutions. This chapter discusses the benefits of diversity and inclusion, as well as strategies for creating a diverse and inclusive workplace. By embracing diversity, organizations can leverage the unique strengths of their employees and drive ethical business growth.

Finally, effective communication is a cornerstone of positive social dynamics. Clear and transparent communication fosters trust, reduces misunderstandings, and promotes collaboration. This chapter provides insights into various communication techniques, such as active listening, feedback, and conflict resolution, that are essential for building strong relationships and driving innovation. By prioritizing effective communication, organizations can create a cohesive and dynamic work environment.

4

Chapter 4: The Role of Ethical Decision-Making in Business Growth

Ethical decision-making is crucial for the sustainable growth and success of any organization. In an increasingly complex and competitive business landscape, companies must navigate a myriad of ethical dilemmas and make decisions that align with their values and principles. This chapter explores the role of ethical decision-making in business growth and provides practical frameworks for making ethical choices.

At the heart of ethical decision-making is the concept of moral reasoning. Moral reasoning involves evaluating the potential consequences of different actions and making choices that uphold ethical standards. This chapter discusses various ethical frameworks, such as utilitarianism, deontology, and virtue ethics, that can guide decision-making processes. By applying these frameworks, leaders can make informed and ethical decisions that contribute to the long-term success of their organizations.

Furthermore, transparency and accountability are essential components of ethical decision-making. Organizations must be transparent about their decision-making processes and hold themselves accountable for their actions. This chapter examines the importance of transparency and accountability in building trust with stakeholders and maintaining a positive reputation. By prioritizing transparency and accountability, organizations can demonstrate their commitment to ethical business practices.

In addition, this chapter explores the role of stakeholder engagement in ethical decision-making. Engaging with stakeholders, including employees, customers, suppliers, and communities, ensures that diverse perspectives are considered in the decision-making process. This chapter provides strategies for effective stakeholder engagement, such as conducting regular consultations, fostering open dialogue, and addressing stakeholder concerns. By involving stakeholders in decision-making, organizations can make more ethical and inclusive choices.

Lastly, ethical decision-making is an ongoing process that requires continuous reflection and improvement. Organizations must regularly evaluate their ethical frameworks and decision-making processes to address emerging challenges and opportunities. This chapter encourages leaders to create a culture of ethical reflection and learning, where employees are empowered to raise ethical concerns and contribute to ethical business growth.

5

Chapter 5: Building an Ethical Culture

Creating an ethical culture within an organization is essential for fostering innovation and sustainable growth. An ethical culture is characterized by a shared commitment to ethical principles and values, which guide decision-making and behavior at all levels. This chapter explores the elements of an ethical culture and provides strategies for cultivating and maintaining it.

One of the foundational elements of an ethical culture is a clear and well-communicated set of values and ethical standards. These values serve as a guiding framework for employees, helping them navigate complex situations and make ethical choices. This chapter discusses the importance of developing and articulating these values and provides practical tips for embedding them into the organization's policies, practices, and daily operations. By consistently reinforcing these values, organizations can create a culture of integrity and accountability.

Leadership plays a crucial role in shaping and sustaining an ethical culture. Ethical leaders lead by example, demonstrating ethical behavior in their actions and decisions. This chapter examines the characteristics of ethical leadership and provides insights into how leaders can inspire and motivate their teams to uphold ethical standards. By fostering an environment of trust and respect, ethical leaders can encourage employees to embrace the organization's values and contribute to its ethical culture.

Moreover, this chapter explores the importance of ethical training and education in building an ethical culture. Regular training programs can equip employees with the knowledge and skills needed to recognize and address ethical dilemmas. This chapter provides strategies for designing and implementing effective ethical training programs, including case studies, role-playing, and interactive workshops. By investing in ethical education, organizations can empower their employees to make ethical decisions and act with integrity.

Lastly, creating an ethical culture requires ongoing evaluation and improvement. Organizations must regularly assess their ethical culture and identify areas for enhancement. This chapter discusses various methods for evaluating ethical culture, such as employee surveys, ethical audits, and feedback mechanisms. By continuously monitoring and improving their ethical culture, organizations can ensure that they remain aligned with their values and mission.

6

Chapter 6: The Intersection of Emotional Intelligence and Social Dynamics

The intersection of emotional intelligence (EI) and social dynamics is a critical area for understanding and driving ethical business growth. EI enables individuals to navigate social dynamics effectively, fostering positive relationships and collaboration. This chapter explores how the interplay between EI and social dynamics contributes to innovation and ethical decision-making.

One of the key ways in which EI influences social dynamics is through the development of strong interpersonal relationships. Leaders with high EI can build trust and rapport with their teams, creating a supportive and inclusive work environment. This chapter discusses various strategies for leveraging EI to strengthen relationships, such as active listening, empathy, and effective communication. By enhancing their EI, leaders can positively impact social dynamics and drive ethical innovation.

Furthermore, EI plays a crucial role in conflict resolution and negotiation. Conflicts are inevitable in any workplace, but how they are managed can significantly impact the organization's culture and innovation efforts. This chapter examines the role of EI in resolving conflicts and reaching mutually beneficial agreements. By applying EI skills, such as emotional regulation and perspective-taking, leaders can address conflicts in a constructive and ethical manner, fostering a positive and collaborative work environment.

Moreover, this chapter explores the impact of social dynamics on emotional well-being. Positive social interactions and relationships can enhance emotional well-being and job satisfaction, leading to increased productivity and creativity. This chapter provides insights into creating a work environment that supports emotional well-being through positive social dynamics, such as team-building activities, recognition programs, and inclusive practices. By prioritizing emotional well-being, organizations can create a thriving and innovative workforce.

Lastly, this chapter discusses the importance of emotional intelligence in leadership development. As organizations grow and evolve, developing emotionally intelligent leaders becomes essential for sustaining ethical business growth. This chapter provides strategies for integrating EI into leadership development programs, including coaching, mentoring, and experiential learning. By nurturing emotionally intelligent leaders, organizations can drive ethical innovation and create a positive impact on their stakeholders.

7

Chapter 7: The Importance of Trust in Ethical Business Growth

Trust is the foundation upon which successful and ethical businesses are built. It is the bedrock of relationships with customers, employees, investors, and other stakeholders. This chapter explores the role of trust in ethical business growth and provides strategies for building and maintaining trust.

Trust is earned through consistent ethical behavior and transparency. Organizations that demonstrate honesty, reliability, and integrity in their actions build trust with their stakeholders. This chapter discusses the importance of transparency in business practices, such as open communication, accountability, and ethical reporting. By being transparent, organizations can create a sense of trust and loyalty among their stakeholders.

Moreover, trust is reinforced through ethical leadership. Leaders who prioritize trust-building and lead by example inspire confidence and loyalty in their teams. This chapter examines various leadership practices that promote trust, such as ethical decision-making, effective communication, and recognizing and addressing employee concerns. By fostering a culture of trust, leaders can create an environment where innovation and ethical growth thrive.

Furthermore, this chapter explores the impact of trust on customer relationships. Customers are more likely to engage with and support businesses they trust. This chapter provides insights into building trust with customers through ethical marketing, customer-centric practices, and delivering on promises. By prioritizing customer trust, organizations can enhance customer loyalty and drive sustainable business growth.

Lastly, maintaining trust requires continuous effort and vigilance. Organizations must be proactive in addressing ethical challenges and ensuring that their actions align with their values. This chapter discusses various strategies for monitoring and maintaining trust, such as regular ethical audits, stakeholder feedback, and continuous improvement. By committing to ethical practices and building trust, organizations can achieve long-term success and growth.

8

Chapter 8: Ethical Innovation in a Globalized World

In a globalized world, businesses face unique ethical challenges and opportunities. As organizations expand their operations across borders, they must navigate diverse cultural, legal, and ethical landscapes. This chapter explores the importance of ethical innovation in a globalized world and provides strategies for addressing global ethical challenges.

One of the key challenges of global business is respecting and understanding cultural differences. This chapter discusses the importance of cultural sensitivity and provides practical tips for fostering cross-cultural understanding and collaboration. By embracing cultural diversity, organizations can enhance their innovation efforts and create ethical solutions that resonate with diverse markets.

Moreover, this chapter examines the role of corporate social responsibility (CSR) in global business. CSR involves integrating ethical considerations into business practices and contributing to the well-being of society and the environment. This chapter provides insights into designing and implementing effective CSR programs that address global challenges, such as climate change, poverty, and human rights. By prioritizing CSR, organizations can create positive social impact and drive ethical business growth.

Furthermore, this chapter explores the importance of ethical supply chain management. As businesses operate in a globalized economy, they must ensure that their supply chains are ethical and sustainable. This chapter discusses various strategies for promoting ethical supply chains, such as supplier audits, fair labor practices, and environmental sustainability. By ensuring that their supply chains align with their ethical values, organizations can build trust with stakeholders and drive ethical innovation.

Lastly, this chapter addresses the role of global partnerships and collaborations in ethical innovation. Collaborating with international partners can provide new perspectives, resources, and opportunities for innovation. This chapter provides strategies for building and maintaining ethical global partnerships, including clear communication, shared values, and mutual respect. By fostering ethical global collaborations, organizations can drive innovation and create positive impact on a global scale.

9

Chapter 9: Ethical Marketing and Branding

Ethical marketing and branding are essential for building trust and loyalty among customers. In an era where consumers are increasingly conscious of the ethical practices of the brands they support, businesses must prioritize transparency, honesty, and responsibility in their marketing efforts. This chapter explores the principles of ethical marketing and provides strategies for developing ethical branding.

Ethical marketing involves promoting products and services in a way that is truthful, transparent, and respectful of consumers. This chapter discusses the importance of accurate and honest advertising, avoiding deceptive practices, and ensuring that marketing messages align with the organization's values. By adhering to ethical marketing principles, businesses can build trust with their customers and create a positive brand image.

Moreover, ethical branding goes beyond marketing to encompass the overall identity and reputation of the organization. This chapter examines the role of brand values and mission in shaping ethical branding. By clearly articulating their ethical values and incorporating them into their branding efforts, organizations can differentiate themselves in the market and attract ethically-minded consumers. This chapter provides practical tips for communicating brand values through various channels, such as social media, packaging, and customer service.

Furthermore, this chapter explores the impact of ethical branding on customer loyalty and advocacy. When consumers perceive a brand as ethical and trustworthy, they are more likely to remain loyal and recommend the brand to others. This chapter provides insights into building and maintaining customer loyalty through ethical practices, such as fair pricing, responsible sourcing, and community engagement. By prioritizing ethical branding, organizations can create a loyal customer base and drive sustainable growth.

Lastly, this chapter discusses the importance of continuous evaluation and improvement in ethical marketing and branding. Organizations must regularly assess their marketing practices and branding strategies to ensure they remain aligned with their ethical values. This chapter provides strategies for conducting ethical audits, seeking customer feedback, and making necessary adjustments. By committing to ethical marketing and branding, organizations can build a strong and positive reputation that supports long-term success.

10

Chapter 10: The Role of Corporate Governance in Ethical Innovation

Corporate governance plays a critical role in ensuring that organizations operate ethically and responsibly. Effective corporate governance provides a framework for decision-making, accountability, and oversight, which are essential for ethical innovation and business growth. This chapter explores the principles of corporate governance and their impact on ethical practices.

One of the key principles of corporate governance is accountability. Organizations must establish clear roles and responsibilities for their leaders and employees, ensuring that they are accountable for their actions and decisions. This chapter discusses various mechanisms for promoting accountability, such as board oversight, performance evaluations, and transparent reporting. By fostering a culture of accountability, organizations can ensure that ethical standards are upheld and that innovation efforts align with their values.

Moreover, corporate governance involves establishing policies and procedures that guide ethical behavior and decision-making. This chapter examines the importance of developing and implementing ethical policies, such as codes of conduct, conflict of interest policies, and whistleblower protection programs. By providing clear guidelines and expectations, organizations can create a structured environment that supports ethical innovation.

Furthermore, this chapter explores the role of stakeholder engagement in corporate governance. Engaging with stakeholders, including shareholders, employees, customers, and communities, ensures that diverse perspectives are considered in decision-making processes. This chapter provides strategies for effective stakeholder engagement, such as regular consultations, transparent communication, and addressing stakeholder concerns. By involving stakeholders in corporate governance, organizations can make more informed and ethical decisions.

Lastly, this chapter discusses the importance of continuous improvement in corporate governance. Organizations must regularly evaluate their governance structures and practices to address emerging challenges and opportunities. This chapter provides strategies for conducting governance assessments, seeking feedback, and making necessary adjustments. By committing to effective corporate governance, organizations can drive ethical innovation and achieve sustainable growth.

11

Chapter 11: Ethical Challenges in the Digital Age

The digital age has brought unprecedented opportunities for innovation, but it has also introduced new ethical challenges. As organizations leverage digital technologies to drive growth and efficiency, they must navigate complex ethical issues related to data privacy, cybersecurity, and artificial intelligence. This chapter explores the ethical challenges of the digital age and provides strategies for addressing them.

One of the most pressing ethical concerns in the digital age is data privacy. Organizations collect and process vast amounts of data, including personal information, to enhance their products and services. This chapter discusses the importance of protecting data privacy and adhering to data protection regulations, such as the General Data Protection Regulation (GDPR). By prioritizing data privacy, organizations can build trust with their customers and avoid legal and reputational risks.

Moreover, cybersecurity is a critical ethical issue in the digital age. Cyber threats, such as hacking, data breaches, and ransomware attacks, pose significant risks to organizations and their stakeholders. This chapter examines the importance of implementing robust cybersecurity measures to protect sensitive information and ensure the integrity of digital systems. By adopting ethical cybersecurity practices, organizations can safeguard their assets and maintain stakeholder trust.

Furthermore, the rise of artificial intelligence (AI) presents unique ethical challenges. AI technologies have the potential to revolutionize industries, but they also raise concerns about bias, transparency, and accountability. This chapter explores the ethical implications of AI and provides strategies for developing and deploying AI systems responsibly. By prioritizing ethical considerations in AI development, organizations can mitigate risks and harness the benefits of AI for ethical innovation.

Lastly, this chapter discusses the role of digital ethics in guiding ethical behavior in the digital age. Digital ethics encompasses the principles and values that govern the use of digital technologies. This chapter provides insights into developing a digital ethics framework, including ethical guidelines, policies, and training programs. By embedding digital ethics into their operations, organizations can navigate the ethical challenges of the digital age and drive ethical business growth.

12

Chapter 12: Ethical Leadership in Times of Crisis

In times of crisis, ethical leadership is more important than ever. Crises, whether they are economic, environmental, or social, test the resilience and integrity of organizations. This chapter explores the role of ethical leadership in navigating crises and provides strategies for leading with integrity during challenging times.

One of the key aspects of ethical leadership in times of crisis is transparency. Leaders must communicate openly and honestly with their stakeholders, providing accurate information and managing expectations. This chapter discusses the importance of transparent communication and provides practical tips for effectively communicating during a crisis. By being transparent, leaders can build trust and credibility with their stakeholders.

Moreover, ethical leadership in times of crisis involves making difficult decisions that prioritize the well-being of stakeholders. This chapter examines the role of ethical decision-making during crises, including the importance of considering the long-term impact of decisions and balancing the needs of different stakeholders. By making ethical choices, leaders can navigate crises with integrity and protect the organization's reputation.

Furthermore, this chapter explores the importance of empathy and compassion in ethical leadership during crises. Leaders who demonstrate empathy can understand and address the concerns and needs of their stakeholders, fostering a sense of solidarity and support. This chapter provides strategies for cultivating empathy and compassion, including active listening, emotional support, and inclusive decision-making. By leading with empathy, leaders can create a positive and resilient organizational culture.

Lastly, ethical leadership in times of crisis requires resilience and adaptability. Leaders must be able to navigate uncertainty and change, while staying true to their values and principles. This chapter discusses the importance of building resilience and provides strategies for developing adaptive leadership skills. By fostering resilience and adaptability, leaders can guide their organizations through crises and emerge stronger and more ethical.

13

Chapter 13: Innovation and Sustainability

Sustainability is increasingly becoming a focal point for modern businesses as they seek to balance profitability with environmental stewardship and social responsibility. This chapter explores the intersection of innovation and sustainability, highlighting the importance of integrating sustainable practices into business operations to drive long-term ethical growth.

Innovation in sustainability involves developing new products, services, and processes that minimize negative environmental impact and promote resource efficiency. This chapter discusses various strategies for sustainable innovation, such as adopting circular economy principles, investing in renewable energy, and reducing waste. By prioritizing sustainability, organizations can create innovative solutions that address global challenges and contribute to a healthier planet.

Moreover, this chapter examines the role of sustainability in enhancing brand reputation and customer loyalty. Consumers are increasingly favoring brands that demonstrate a commitment to environmental and social responsibility. This chapter provides insights into communicating sustainability efforts effectively, including transparent reporting, eco-friendly packaging, and community engagement. By showcasing their sustainability initiatives, organizations can build trust and loyalty among ethically-minded consumers.

Furthermore, sustainable innovation requires collaboration and partnerships. This chapter explores the importance of collaborating with stakeholders, such as suppliers, customers, and industry peers, to drive sustainable innovation. By working together, organizations can pool resources, share knowledge, and develop innovative solutions that benefit both business and society.

Lastly, this chapter discusses the role of leadership in driving sustainable innovation. Leaders must champion sustainability initiatives and create a culture that encourages environmental responsibility. This chapter provides strategies for integrating sustainability into leadership development, including setting sustainability goals, providing training, and recognizing and rewarding sustainable practices. By fostering a culture of sustainability, leaders can drive ethical innovation and ensure long-term success.

14

Chapter 14: The Future of Work: Ethical Considerations

The future of work is being shaped by rapid technological advancements, shifting demographics, and evolving societal expectations. As organizations navigate these changes, they must address ethical considerations related to the future of work. This chapter explores the ethical implications of emerging trends and provides strategies for creating a future of work that prioritizes integrity and well-being.

One of the key trends shaping the future of work is automation and artificial intelligence. While these technologies have the potential to increase efficiency and productivity, they also raise concerns about job displacement and inequality. This chapter discusses the ethical implications of automation and AI and provides strategies for managing their impact on the workforce. By prioritizing ethical considerations, organizations can create a future of work that benefits both employees and businesses.

Moreover, the future of work is characterized by increased flexibility and remote work. This chapter examines the ethical challenges and opportunities associated with flexible work arrangements, such as work-life balance, inclusivity, and employee well-being. By adopting ethical practices, such as fair compensation, clear communication, and support for remote workers, organizations can create a positive and inclusive work environment.

Furthermore, diversity and inclusion are critical considerations for the future of work. As the workforce becomes more diverse, organizations must prioritize inclusivity and address biases and discrimination. This chapter provides insights into creating a diverse and inclusive workplace, including strategies for recruiting diverse talent, fostering an inclusive culture, and addressing systemic barriers. By embracing diversity and inclusion, organizations can drive innovation and create a more equitable future of work.

Lastly, this chapter discusses the importance of lifelong learning and development in the future of work. As the nature of work evolves, employees must continuously update their skills and knowledge. This chapter provides strategies for fostering a culture of continuous learning, including offering training programs, encouraging professional development, and supporting career growth. By investing in their employees' development, organizations can create a resilient and adaptable workforce that drives ethical innovation.

15

Chapter 15: The Role of Ethics in Research and Development

Ethics play a vital role in guiding research and development (R&D) processes within organizations. Ethical R&D ensures that innovations are developed responsibly and with consideration for societal impact. This chapter explores the principles of ethical R&D and provides strategies for integrating ethics into the innovation process.

One of the key principles of ethical R&D is integrity. Researchers and developers must adhere to ethical standards, such as honesty, transparency, and accountability, in their work. This chapter discusses the importance of maintaining research integrity, including avoiding plagiarism, ensuring accurate data reporting, and acknowledging contributions. By upholding integrity, organizations can build trust and credibility in their innovations.

Moreover, ethical R&D involves considering the potential impact of innovations on society and the environment. This chapter examines the importance of conducting thorough ethical assessments and risk evaluations before proceeding with new developments. By identifying and addressing potential ethical concerns early in the R&D process, organizations can mitigate risks and ensure that their innovations contribute positively to society.

Furthermore, this chapter explores the role of stakeholder engagement in ethical R&D. Involving stakeholders in the R&D process ensures that diverse perspectives are considered and that innovations align with societal needs and values. This chapter provides strategies for effective stakeholder engagement, such as participatory research, public consultations, and collaboration with academic and industry partners. By engaging stakeholders, organizations can enhance the ethical and social relevance of their innovations.

Lastly, ethical R&D requires continuous learning and improvement. Organizations must stay informed about emerging ethical challenges and best practices in their fields. This chapter discusses the importance of fostering a culture of ethical reflection and learning, including providing ongoing ethical training and creating platforms for ethical discussions. By prioritizing ethical R&D, organizations can drive responsible and sustainable innovation.

16

Chapter 16: The Role of Ethics in Corporate Strategy

Ethical considerations are integral to the development and implementation of corporate strategies. Organizations that prioritize ethics in their strategic planning processes are better positioned to achieve long-term success and positive societal impact. This chapter explores the role of ethics in corporate strategy and provides insights into integrating ethical principles into strategic decision-making.

One of the key aspects of ethical corporate strategy is aligning business goals with ethical values. Organizations must ensure that their strategic objectives are consistent with their commitment to ethical behavior and social responsibility. This chapter discusses various approaches for aligning corporate strategy with ethical values, such as incorporating sustainability goals, prioritizing stakeholder well-being, and adhering to ethical standards in business operations. By aligning their strategies with ethical principles, organizations can build trust and credibility with their stakeholders.

Moreover, ethical corporate strategy involves making decisions that consider the long-term impact on society and the environment. This chapter examines the importance of incorporating ethical considerations into strategic decision-making processes, including conducting ethical impact assessments and considering the broader societal implications of business decisions. By adopting a long-term perspective, organizations can make strategic choices that contribute to ethical growth and sustainability.

Furthermore, this chapter explores the role of corporate governance in ensuring ethical corporate strategy. Effective governance structures provide oversight and accountability, ensuring that ethical considerations are integrated into strategic planning. This chapter provides insights into establishing robust governance frameworks, such as forming ethics committees, implementing ethical policies, and conducting regular ethical reviews. By strengthening governance, organizations can ensure that their strategies are guided by ethical principles.

Lastly, this chapter discusses the importance of ethical leadership in driving corporate strategy. Leaders play a crucial role in setting the ethical tone and guiding strategic direction. This chapter provides strategies for fostering ethical leadership, including providing ethical training, encouraging ethical decision-making, and recognizing and rewarding ethical behavior. By promoting ethical leadership, organizations can create a culture of integrity that supports ethical corporate strategy.

17

Chapter 17: Ethical Business Growth: A Roadmap for the Future

The future of business growth lies in the integration of ethical principles into all aspects of operations and decision-making. This concluding chapter provides a roadmap for organizations seeking to achieve ethical business growth, drawing on the key insights and strategies discussed throughout the book.

One of the fundamental pillars of ethical business growth is the commitment to continuous improvement. Organizations must regularly evaluate their ethical practices and seek opportunities for enhancement. This chapter emphasizes the importance of fostering a culture of ethical reflection and learning, encouraging employees to engage in ongoing ethical education and discussions. By prioritizing continuous improvement, organizations can stay ahead of emerging ethical challenges and drive sustainable growth.

Moreover, ethical business growth requires a holistic approach that considers the well-being of all stakeholders. This chapter discusses the importance of adopting a stakeholder-centric perspective, ensuring that business decisions consider the interests and needs of employees, customers, suppliers, communities, and the environment. By embracing stakeholder inclusivity, organizations can build strong relationships and create positive social impact.

Furthermore, innovation and ethics must go hand in hand for ethical business growth. Organizations should strive to develop innovative solutions that address societal challenges and promote sustainability. This chapter provides strategies for fostering ethical innovation, such as adopting sustainable practices, leveraging technology for social good, and engaging in ethical R&D. By integrating ethics into their innovation processes, organizations can drive meaningful and responsible growth.

Lastly, ethical business growth is a journey that requires strong leadership and commitment. Leaders must champion ethical values and inspire their teams to uphold high ethical standards. This chapter discusses the role of ethical leadership in guiding organizations towards ethical growth, including setting a positive example, fostering a culture of integrity, and recognizing and rewarding ethical behavior. By prioritizing ethical leadership, organizations can create a future where innovation and integrity go hand in hand.

18

Chapter 18: Implementing Ethical Standards Across Global Operations

As businesses expand globally, maintaining consistent ethical standards across diverse geographical regions becomes increasingly important. This chapter explores the challenges and opportunities of implementing ethical standards in a global context and provides strategies for ensuring ethical consistency.

One of the key challenges of global operations is navigating different cultural norms and legal frameworks. This chapter discusses the importance of cultural sensitivity and legal compliance in maintaining ethical standards. By understanding and respecting local customs and regulations, organizations can ensure that their global operations align with their ethical values.

Moreover, this chapter examines the role of corporate governance in maintaining ethical standards across global operations. Effective governance structures provide oversight and accountability, ensuring that ethical considerations are integrated into decision-making processes. This chapter provides insights into establishing robust governance frameworks, such as forming ethics committees, implementing ethical policies, and conducting regular ethical reviews. By strengthening governance, organizations can ensure that their global operations are guided by ethical principles.

Furthermore, this chapter explores the importance of training and education in promoting ethical standards globally. Regular training programs can equip employees with the knowledge and skills needed to recognize and address ethical dilemmas. This chapter provides strategies for designing and implementing effective ethical training programs, including case studies, role-playing, and interactive workshops. By investing in ethical education, organizations can empower their employees to uphold ethical standards across all regions.

Lastly, this chapter discusses the role of communication in maintaining ethical standards globally. Clear and transparent communication fosters trust, reduces misunderstandings, and promotes collaboration. This chapter provides insights into various communication techniques, such as active listening, feedback, and conflict resolution, that are essential for building strong relationships and driving ethical innovation. By prioritizing effective communication, organizations can create a cohesive and dynamic work environment.

19

Chapter 19: Measuring the Impact of Ethical Practices

Measuring the impact of ethical practices is essential for understanding their effectiveness and making informed decisions for continuous improvement. This chapter explores various methods for evaluating the impact of ethical practices and provides strategies for leveraging data to drive ethical innovation.

One of the key methods for measuring the impact of ethical practices is through performance metrics and key performance indicators (KPIs). This chapter discusses the importance of selecting relevant KPIs that align with the organization's ethical goals and values. By tracking and analyzing these metrics, organizations can assess the effectiveness of their ethical practices and identify areas for improvement.

Moreover, stakeholder feedback is a valuable source of information for measuring the impact of ethical practices. This chapter examines various methods for collecting and analyzing stakeholder feedback, such as surveys, interviews, and focus groups. By engaging with stakeholders and incorporating their perspectives, organizations can gain a comprehensive understanding of the impact of their ethical practices.

Furthermore, ethical audits are an important tool for evaluating the effectiveness of ethical practices. This chapter discusses the process of conducting ethical audits, including setting audit objectives, identifying areas of focus, and developing audit criteria. By regularly conducting ethical audits, organizations can ensure that their practices align with their values and identify opportunities for improvement.

Lastly, this chapter explores the role of continuous improvement in driving ethical innovation. Organizations must regularly evaluate their ethical practices and seek opportunities for enhancement. This chapter provides strategies for fostering a culture of continuous improvement, including encouraging employee feedback, providing ongoing ethical training, and recognizing and rewarding ethical behavior. By prioritizing continuous improvement, organizations can stay ahead of emerging ethical challenges and drive sustainable growth.

20

Chapter 20: The Future of Ethical Innovation

The future of ethical innovation lies in the continued integration of ethical principles into all aspects of business operations and decision-making. This concluding chapter provides a roadmap for organizations seeking to achieve ethical business growth, drawing on the key insights and strategies discussed throughout the book.

One of the fundamental pillars of ethical innovation is the commitment to continuous improvement. Organizations must regularly evaluate their ethical practices and seek opportunities for enhancement. This chapter emphasizes the importance of fostering a culture of ethical reflection and learning, encouraging employees to engage in ongoing ethical education and discussions. By prioritizing continuous improvement, organizations can stay ahead of emerging ethical challenges and drive sustainable growth.

Moreover, ethical innovation requires a holistic approach that considers the well-being of all stakeholders. This chapter discusses the importance of adopting a stakeholder-centric perspective, ensuring that business decisions consider the interests and needs of employees, customers, suppliers, communities, and the environment. By embracing stakeholder inclusivity, organizations can build strong relationships and create positive social impact.

Furthermore, innovation and ethics must go hand in hand for ethical business growth. Organizations should strive to develop innovative solutions that address societal challenges and promote sustainability. This chapter provides strategies for fostering ethical innovation, such as adopting sustainable practices, leveraging technology for social good, and engaging in ethical R&D. By integrating ethics into their innovation processes, organizations can drive meaningful and responsible growth.

Lastly, ethical business growth is a journey that requires strong leadership and commitment. Leaders must champion ethical values and inspire their teams to uphold high ethical standards. This chapter discusses the role of ethical leadership in guiding organizations towards ethical growth, including setting a positive example, fostering a culture of integrity, and recognizing and rewarding ethical behavior. By prioritizing ethical leadership, organizations can create a future where innovation and integrity go hand in hand.

Book Description

"**Innovating with Integrity: Emotional Intelligence, Social Dynamics, and Ethical Business Growth**" is a comprehensive guide to understanding the interplay between ethical principles, emotional intelligence, and social dynamics in driving sustainable and responsible business innovation. This book delves into the core values that underpin ethical leadership and provides practical strategies for fostering an ethical culture within organizations. By integrating real-world examples, actionable insights, and reflective exercises, this book empowers leaders and professionals to navigate complex ethical challenges and create positive social impact.

www.ingramcontent.com/pod-product-compliance
Lightning Source LLC
LaVergne TN
LVHW020455080526
838202LV00057B/5965